Trapeze

Trapeze

POEMS

Deborah Digges

ALFRED A. KNOPF
New York 2010

THIS IS A BORZOI BOOK
PUBLISHED BY ALFRED A. KNOPF

Copyright © 2004 by Deborah Digges

www.randomhouse.com/knopf/poetry

Owing to space limitations, permissions
will be found following the acknowledgments.

Knopf, Borzoi Books, and the colophon are registered
trademarks of Random House, Inc.

Library of Congress Cataloging-in-Publication Data

Digges, Deborah.
Trapeze : poems / by Deborah Digges.
p.   cm.
ISBN 0-375-71021-3
I. Title.

PS3554.I3922T73 2004
811'.54—dc22   2003055759

Printed in the United States of America
Published March 19, 2004
First paperback edition September 13, 2005
Second Printing, June 2010

For my darling Frank and for my children

Could there be those who see us off at the beginning, never to know what will become of us, must let us go. Do they hold on to shadows pressed like flowers in a book—set in their windows like sea-glass vials of birthing waters. Beyond a field. The stones that marked each grave I moved myself. Heaved them and rolled them into place. Felt the good ache across my shoulders as I brushed my hair or washed my soul's garments so recently returned to me. Let me not turn away. What I am is all that I can carry.

CONTENTS

Trapeze

WINTER BARN

A light slant snow dragging the fields, a counter-wind
where the edges of the barn frayed worlds,

blurred outside in. This is what my love could give me
instead of children—the dusk as presence, mothlike,

and with a moth's dust colored flickering stall by stall,
some empty now, certain gone to slaughter, driven north

in open trucks over potholed, frozen roads.
Such a hard ride to bloodlet, blankness, the stalls' stone

floors hosed out, yet damp, the urine reek not quite
muffled with fresh hay, trough water still giving back lantern

light like ponds at nightfall. Sheep lay steaming, cloud
in cloud. The barn cat slept among last summer's lambs, black-

faced, apart, relieved of their mothers. We made our way,
my dogs and I, to say hello to the Yorkshire sow

named Kora, who heaved herself up to greet us,
let the dogs lick her oiled snout smeared with feed,

while I scratched her forehead. Kora of the swineherds
fallen with Persephone, perhaps in hell a bride's only company.

Prodigal, planetary, Kora's great-spined, strict-bristled body
wore the black mud of a cold, righteous creation,

burrs and mugwort plastered at the gates.
Days her smell stayed with us. The last time we saw her

the plaque bearing her name was gone. Maybe she would be mated.
Sparrows sailed the barn's doomed girth, forsaken,

therefore free. They lit on rafters crossing the west windows
that flared at sunset like a furnace fed on stars.

It fell to me to tell the bees,
though I had wanted another duty—
to be the scribbler at his death,
there chart the third day's quickening.
But fate said no, it falls to you
to tell the bees, the middle daughter.
So it was written at your birth.
I wanted to keep the fire, working
the constant arranging and shifting
of the coals blown flaring,
my cheeks flushed red,
my bed laid down before the fire,
myself anonymous among the strangers
there who'd come and go.
But destiny said no. It falls
to you to tell the bees, it said.
I wanted to be the one to wash his linens,
boiling the death-soiled sheets,
using the waters for my tea.
I might have been the one to seal
his solitude with mud and thatch and string,
the webs he parted every morning,
the hounds' hair combed from brushes,
the dust swept into piles with sparrows' feathers.
Who makes the laws that live
inside the brick and mortar of a name,
selects the seeds, garden or wild,
brings forth the foliage grown up around it
through drought or blight or blossom,
the honey darkening in the bitter years,

the combs like funeral lace or wedding veils
steeped in oak gall and rainwater,
sequined of rent wings.
And so arrayed I set out, this once
obedient, toward the hives' domed skeps
on evening's hill, five tombs alight.
I thought I heard the thrash and moaning
of confinement, beyond the century,
a calling across dreams,
as if asked to make haste just out of sleep.
I knelt and waited.
The voice that found me gave the news.
Up flew the bees toward his orchards.

Ponds are spring-fed, lakes run off rivers.
Here souls pass, not one deified,
and sometimes this is terrible to know
three floors below the street, where light drinks the world,
siphoned like music through portals.
How fed, that dark, the octaves framed faceless.
A memory of water.
The trees more beautiful not themselves.
Souls who have passed here, tired, brightening.
Dumpsters of linen, empty
gurneys along corridors to parking garages.
Who wonders, is it morning?
Who washes these blankets?
Can I not be the greeter of souls?
What's to be done with the envelopes of hair?
If the inlets are frozen, can I walk across?
When I look down into myself to see a scattering of birds,
do I put on the new garments?
On which side of the river should I wait?

LILACS

Let's say for that time
I was an instrument forbidding music.
That spring no thief of fire.
I tapped from the source a self sick of love,
and then beyond sickness,
an invalid of my loathing.
Yes, loathing put me to bed each night
and burned my dreams,
in the morning woke me with strong coffee.
And this was loathing's greeting—
Get up. Drink.
All this in spite of the lilacs returning,
their odor the odor of life everlasting,
another year,
another season onward, another spring.
But they bloomed of a sudden pale in unison
like lifeboats rowing into dawn,
the passengers gone mad, exhausted in the open,
even the wives, the mothers
rescued for their children,
their lives, believe me, not their own.
Boats full of lilacs drifting thus,
each grayish bush against my gray house.
But theirs is a short season, a few weeks,
rarely more.
And I was glad to be rid of them,
rid of a thing that could touch in me
what might be called "mercy."
See how one's lips must kiss to make the *m,*
touch tongue to back of teeth and smile.

8

Pity's swept clean and conscious,
an upstairs room whose floors resound,
but mercy's an asylum,
a house sliding forever out to sea.
As if I were expected to wade out into the yard each night
and swing a lantern!
And just this morning, still early into autumn,
I noticed how the lilacs had set themselves on fire.
As for me, I have my privacy.
It's mine I might have killed for.
I have my solitude,
the face of the beloved like a room locked in time,
and when I look back I am not there.
It's as if the lilacs martyred themselves,
the stories of their journey
embellished or misread
or lacking a true bard, a song associate,
something with starlight in it,
blue lilac starlight
and the sound of dipping oars.
I could sing it for them now,
make it up as I go along,
a detailed, useless lyric among shipwrecking green.
In my heart is the surprise of dusk come early
to ancient shapes like cairns,
the cold rising vast, these episodes
of silence like eternity.
Sing with me a siren song,
a ferryman song.
Sing for the dead lilacs.

TRAPEZE

See how the first dark takes the city in its arms
and carries it into what yesterday we called the future.

O, the dying are such acrobats.
Here you must take a boat from one day to the next,

or clutch the girders of the bridge, hand over hand.
But they are sailing like a pendulum between eternity and evening,

diving, recovering, balancing the air.
Who can tell at this hour seabirds from starlings,

wind from revolving doors or currents off the river.
Some are as children on swings pumping higher and higher.

Don't call them back, don't call them in for supper.
See, they leave scuff marks like jet trails on the sky.

The former tenants kept birds they let fly loose through rooms whose
windows overlooked the cemetery. What came up with the heat and
flies in winter put pepper in the air, a smell not unfamiliar if you've
ever picked up feathers in the woods and run them along your face, or
found a nest and put it under glass. Droppings filigreed the fixtures,
rained in the soapstone sink where God knows what got washed over
the years. I don't remember cooking there, only getting a drink of
water mornings. Once on my way to bed my watch dropped from my
wrist, the moon glass shattering on the stairs. I sat down on the
landing to touch the naked face, the brittle golden hands. It would
have been the perfect place to die. Too perfect, actually. I must have
known it then. More likely thought that someone would have won.
The man, but something more huge behind him. Some wrong eternity
that wouldn't budge, like trying to move a wardrobe or a safe, only to
feel how light I was. All I could think to do was paint a wall white.
Shame banks on evidence, but who'll go looking for dead canaries?
Nor is remembering like taking a book down from the shelf to find old
keepsakes fluttering out. With each gesture of faith, light off the
blade. Say someone left behind a tray of bones, the songs that found
me there beyond my hearing, and I to learn each fingering. You've seen
bright scores of ribbon ripped out of a cassette, a quickening, ruined,
undulating flash up from the gutters where the snow's thawed, the
dark waters running, or wind-strung, raining from the trees, voice
and the instrument imprinted, bannered, banished, hopelessly
tangled, soon to be swallowed by foliage.

We were too strange for him, the mole.
All morning I watched the cat
dance at the trapdoor to his crypt,
till I forgot to watch, at which moment
she dragged him up inside our ethers,
his webbed feet wild swimming. He
flailed. A sad gauntlet, his star nose
limply flung against my palm, the air.
Instinct called behind me almost
too far away to hear—cover him
who cannot right himself!—and made
of my hands a hermit's hovel,
looked in and in, set his house down
when it was safe, mole hobbling
under the leaves' low roofs toward
private entrance to an old world's
root-bound basements unpacked of sand
and bone, his tiny mines worm-warm
against the whoosh and trickle
at bedrock, channels far above of primal
waters. There are few things worth
saving now that either cannot save
themselves or were better lost,
winter coming on, nevertheless may
wash up here, and who knows which being
takes advantage. Who remembers of a season
what becomes of these, mortal or otherwise,
unless there be no otherwise. The light
of earth says simply gone, yes.
As for your dead, they will not be

returning. The leafless burial woods fill
with brilliant brutal light. How few
you've loved toward posterity. You only
recognized each other. Who wouldn't envy
the mole his nature, old fossor,
Charon's shadow crossing over.
Under the sky behold such absence,
its soul-sheen hearth's ashes,
and threshold-close, the voice inside
the door. I would be proud to wear
a gown of moleskins like a seal,
and sun-grazed merely, dive headlong there.

SEERSUCKER SUIT

To the curator of the museum, to the exhibition of fathers,
to the next room from this closet of trousers
and trousers, full sail the walnut hangers of shirts,
O the great ghost ships of his shoes.
Through the racks and the riggings,
belt buckles ringing and coins in coat pockets
and moths that fly up from the black woolen remnants,
his smell like a kiss blown through hallways of cedar,
the shape of him locked in his burial clothes,
his voice tucked deep in his name,
his keys and the bells to his heart,
I am passing his light blue seersucker suit
with one grass-stained knee,
and a white shirt, clean boxers, clean socks, a handkerchief.

THE RAINBOW BRIDGE IN THE PAINTING OF THE SUNG DYNASTY

For the tying together of two ends of the hemp cord
and the harvesting of bamboo forests,
for the month of rains,

the river flooding,
and the scaffolding reflected in the water,

for the ghost of what-had-been departing

and the brushfires doused
with opium and urine,

for the poles that found the bottom of the river
and the colors in their order nine times braided,

for the hundred roses fed into the pyre
and the footbridge strung onshore to learn the netting,
for the crush of berries,
blood, and coal, and two boats

anchored in the middle of the river,
for the boar's-hair brushes
dipped into the water and the greater rise and thrust

of the abutments, for the finger-stitch
from beam to arch, and the centuries of mornings stealing pigment,
for the float of granite

boat-shaped pilings and the counter-law in which redundancy
is safety, for time locked in a circle

on the ground and the boat springing a leak
that held the frame,

for the trapeze of hammocks wafting between willows
and the hands knit closer by their weaving,

for the circle of fires that kept away the tigers
and the certain bleed of earth's three colors,
for the spaces between characters
inked right to left

and the other shore each day by dusk
foreshortened, for the distance
inside years of letters written
and the warp of the reverse curve's arc dismantled,

for the moths enclosed,
their wing-dust fingerprinted
and the charting of the light, season by season,

for the weeds
sprouting in the clefts between the pilings
and the dragon's shadow in the keystone lengthening,
for the shift in clouds,

the bridges disappearing
and the strength of the rope of grasses nine times
braided, for the divinities

whereby the four horizons gathered
and the toe of the dragon fixing latitude at sea,

for the spinning of the webs broken each morning

and time looking back from the middle of the river,

for four hands
touching in the shuttling of a string bridge,
and the ox led out across the rainbow.

BOAT

Wind off the small pond where I set my rubber
boat down and climbed in, my child-sized paddle
barely long enough to push off or feather
a rudderless craft. Easier to drift in circles
across the late-March waters, my dogs
wild at the idea of spring's first cold immersions.
Still, they swam out to try to climb aboard,
swamping my little boat until, soaked through,
I paddled back, spilled roaring in the shallows.
Onshore two mothers watched, and their
young children who neither waved nor smiled,
nor I. Distance forgave us, and the babies,
who stood on guard, sticks in their little
hands raised to the pack shaking dry,
running headlong in their direction.
The mothers swept children onto hips
and turned, barely maneuvering behind them
strollers tipping a wreck of bright bottle bags,
toys, blankets, perhaps extra clothes.
Once they looked back to show me myself at fifty,
frightening to them, not yet recognizable, the self-
same, almost, in an old nightmare obsolete,
who might have called out to reassure
as I buried my freezing legs in the sun-warmed
sand and lay back, flanked by three dogs
and a rubber boat. O brilliant, trivial unmooring.

Then he was flying buried, cut from the ice, airlifted through the
    ages of interminable starlight,
dragged like earth's only moon into the cave of caves, imagine,
twenty cables breaking, thirty quadrants sectioning his girth
    pitched sideways under low ceilings.
Here it was spring below the world.
We kept the fires burning, we tied our shadows to our waists
as we beheld a host of grasses forge rivers in his wake,
a steppe land turned to desert, turned to ice, where seas moved in
    and out.
We lay down like children in the yards of auburn hair,
buried our faces to breathe in the second golden growth's
    miraculous musk, odor of mammoth,
and sorted seed from spore, rooted what we could to watch it fail.
The light was poor. We couldn't rest. Smoke from the torches
    burned our eyes,
blackened our faces already mammoth-tarred and mammoth-
    smeared with tears.
Who'd build him back to breathe and die struck flesh then,
threaded the needle, set cells dividing an aberration too huge to
    birth under the sun.
But please don't fall alone into the world again.
We will be old. You couldn't recognize us waving across this arctic
    of remembrance.
Swim toward the dark, swim back to bog, bleed through.
Be once and all. That you have lived, borne out.
What was borne out not to be ours but it was poetry.

MIDSUMMER

His shoulders shook
where he knelt to retch
at the edge of the woods.
I stood there stupid,
bleating his name,
dragging across the gravel
road the cooler full
of lemons, medications.
He lay down after
near the water under
a pine and almost slept.
I sent my heart on
home to greet us.
But as we rose, nations
of swallowtails rose
with us, who'd sought
the shade, the moss
currents of the pond's
stone basements.
They climbed the spiral
air like tiny brides
trailing some lantern
on a stair beyond us,

or wanting us to wear them
there, lit in our hair like
garlands, rode our shoulders.
Back in the car we
watched them spread
a raiment in the road,
midsummer yellow.
I drove while my beloved
walked ahead, herding
the swallowtails into the trees.

We were the host posing as flesh, or just the opposite,
    robber brides,
the mothers of thieves and scoundrels, drifting as clouds drawn
    from Castilian waters,

or the Pleiades most visible at dawn above Mount Helicon,
till we could hear the cricket shuttling of Lachesis' loom.

There browsed among huge wardrobes, trunks, hatboxes,
    everything lashed
down/draped/wedded/moored in cobwebs so luxurious

the west winds starboard shook the spills like the sails of ghost
    ships.
Was it Catullus' dust we swept from the glass counters displaying
    Ladon's leash,

tooth of the she-wolf and locks of her wild boys' hair,
the very rope by which Antigone hanged herself, pink stones

from Aberdour, Sappho's tiara, the many, many broken lyres,
a garbage heap of cell doors off their hinges, curtains rent, at last,
    on all the sonnets.

The three Fates frowned as we tried on hats—Pope Gregory's,
    St. Augustine's, Josephus'.
And still we strode, bowed, genuflected, performed a mock heroics
    of men seeking God.

Then sidestepped that eternity to be the moon pulling sea glass
    from the sea.
And purchased lanterns of the virgins, some from the foolish,
    some the wise,

threw over Dante's boots and John's hair shirt to try on Cleopatra's
    funeral dress.
The robes of the Greek chorus needed mending. Wine stained
    this gown.

I boiled it in green tea. Girded in gold about my waist,
fresh laurels in my hair, it might be just the thing to wear to my
    last marriage.

MY LIFE'S CALLING

My life's calling, setting fires.
Here in a hearth so huge
I can stand inside and shove
the wood around with my
bare hands while church bells
deal the hours down through
the chimney. No more
woodcutter, creel for the fire
or architect, the five staves
pitched like rifles over stone.
But to be *mistro-elemental*.
The flute of clay playing
my breath that riles the flames,
the fire risen to such dreaming
sung once from landlords' attics.
Sung once the broken lyres,
seasoned and green.
Even the few things I might save,
my mother's letters,
locks of my children's hair
here handed over like the keys
to a foreclosure, my robes
remanded, and furniture
dragged out into the yard,

my bedsheets hoisted up the pine,
whereby the house sets sail.
And I am standing on a cliff
above the sea, a paper light,
a lantern. No longer mine
to count the wrecks.
Who rode the ships in ringing,
marrying rock the waters
storm to break the door,
looked through the fire, beheld
a clearing there. This is what
you are. What you've come to.

GUILLOTINE WINDOWS

Fifty brief summers, fifty northeastern
winters have close to petrified the frames
once carefully recessed and rigged with pulleys, though the ropes
have frayed, the weights like clappers dropped inside the walls.

They're called eight-over-twelves, my guillotine windows,
that slam themselves on spring,
and the wooden spoons that prop them up belly like yew bows,
and the empty shampoo bottles *woo,* and the knives, hairbrushes,
shoe trees, books, and jewelry boxes,
all will be ruined soon.

Ring the house that wants it to be winter,
a house for wintering, warn the spirits they'll lose a hand,
a tail sailing in and out of the bell tower

above rue festering, the huge moonlight Scotch broom,
above my rabid gardens, my complicated gardens.

If the body is a temple, surely one's garden is like a mind,
half-seeded by the wind, ready to slip into its own peculiar madness,

the Russian sage awash over the beech roots strangling my pipes,
and the bellwort rampant, foxglove, violets
banked by my Grecian stones, and blue glass totem toads
and china figs, beheaded angels, and shells I've carried back

from different coasts fashioned like Sapphic cliffs.
Someday they'll think this was a lovers' leap,

the cellar of a dried-out public well
into which those fleeing threw what weighed them down—

hair in a locket, keys, rings, Bibles and the flowers pressed
in the Psalms, a doll's head, funeral lace

preserved in the historic leaf rot of a willow,
plum and apple, oak, and two white pines, two sycamores.

I love to imagine someone, say when I'm transplanting
at midnight, finding the remnants of this place.

On my knees in the garden in the dark I can look in the windows
and see fields that will be glacial,
hillsides whereon headstones dwarf and pitch

above a woods from which my floors came flying
in clouds of animal fur and dust and human hair and ash from a
        thousand fires
swept from the hearth, saved until spring—tamped down,
drawn up as color into lilacs.

Once I watched a house taken out to sea.
From that distance it looked like the earth bent down to crown
the ocean and the ocean, rising, thus received the crown
of the house that deified the waves awhile.

Imagine standing alone there at the threshold,
having an ocean as one's garden for a moment, a garden

of enormous green-blue rollers, seabirds, four winds,
    countless clouds!

You can have a good life and not know it.
You can claim that seeing far means seeing into the future,
into the time ahead of you.

But it was all right to have believed in something—
that those you loved, they would outlive you
or simply be here always from time to time,
and you would recognize each other,

take hands and walk through a garden, have a meal together,
talk late into the evening and fall asleep in separate rooms.

See those young selves waving back at shore,
see them running, calling to you, as the walls of the house
break up, pulling from the foundation while the roof
slides sideways, gone, and the windows shatter,

and some float in their frames, float shining whole,
carried out, drifting, windows on the sea.

There are benches outside the bower
on which is written *All spoons be confiscated.*
Here sit the ones who tearfully protest,
others who fight with fists
to keep their spoons,
if only for a little while, for just an hour,
Show us to God, they say,
spoons in our hands.
Show him our lifting spoons now to each other's lips
instead of white flag raised or olive branch.
Such is spoon's fugue, its song of songs,
a rune whose instrument knows
all five fingers, closing and closing
the most mortal of all circles—
mother to child and child to father,
bride to her beloved,
the selfsame to be filled and filled
and licked clean of elixirs.
Clapper to time is spoon, sap-golden,
a chandelier of spoons ringing in the pine,
light-lashed above the garden.
Though the righteous be snatched to heaven upright
in their ascensions,
spoon's palm mirrors our fate, my love,
when we hang batlike over the earth.
O music of pomegranates riven inside the light,
Solomon's spoons ring for the exiles,
we who refuse eternity to keep our spoons.

ICE FISHERMEN

We could walk all the way across, the dogs
and I, snow-deaf January days, the sun
held underwater, the ice a lantern.
So closely bound, degrees of likeness,
whether to build a fire, where squat to smoke,
refill the flask, pee with the dogs among the birches.
I wanted to show you how this wand
of fern, laid sideways on my palm,
becomes a row the trees and their reflections.
I wanted to tell you how we longed to slide
where only months ago I had thrown in sticks
for the dalmatian desperate to swim
straight through quicksilver paths of sun,
and dive, and reappear, as from another time.
Summer or winter, we bristled
when some other car pulled in,
and took the prison road if it was plowed.
If not, the basset's feet would freeze in the deep snow.
There was a field we loved the wind
combed to the bone, but we were drawn
down to the animal *ping* and groan of the ice shifting
and the echo, as if to meet new souls arriving
from islands bare under pines,
little summers of moss, red quills staining silt
in the many inlets of the pond, our white pavilions,

surely the setting for the dreams the dogs chased
in their sleep, the husky whimpering
so loud she'd wake me.
One day we found we weren't alone.
Men with young sons camped on the ice.
They sat on lobster traps around a corkscrewed hole,
and cooked up trout no bigger than my hand.
The dogs ran out to greet them
to be barred by shouts and oars raised at them
and the gulls that swept from the bridge.
We kept to the woods till they had gone,
the ice glowing beneath us,
we who were called for you to wait
and then to witness and make account,
but where and when, the bed empty,
the snows raked golden.
Down the blue broken, reckless stars,
a cistern suck of waters. I kicked the embers
from their fires in there and heard the hiss
and warned the dogs away and we kept moving.

SO LIGHT YOU WERE
I WOULD HAVE CARRIED YOU

So light you were
I would have carried you,
hacked from the ice
a bridge,
you in my arms,
from February into April.
And crossed
above the snow
banked narrowing
the streets, this winter's
tired citizens, the erlking
and his foundling crossing.
Light as you were
I would have carried you
from the room
of your death back
to our room,
climbed back,
crawled up the stairs
to our bed.
From February into

April, hid in your arms
in the woods'
frantic *please*.
Light as we were.
And could be carried out
on a float of last year's
leaves
and bracken thaw
rinsing the tide pools.
So light you were.
I would have carried you
from February
into April.

Rain through the skylights ruined the books, a month of rains. He
packed his things and left for good. The books were monsters. Pried
from the shelves they burst their bindings, the classics no less
grotesque, first editions. Old criminals all, beloved pile of ruined,
heavy books, stripped and hosed down, herded to a commons, some
stumbling without their trusses. Their gases steamed the windows,
and a strange sheeny filament like hair, a sour aquatic mess rose from
the pile, found shape above the books and breathed, old fish eyes
filming over. And then on any of those summer nights you could hear
snatches of irrational conspiracies. And such profanities up from the
barracks. The meek grew cunning, exchanging hats with fate, while
the devout lunged through the bars at every dream. Who could sleep
for the racket of so many plucked, unstrung? Priceless instruments
in the hands of drunkards. Mornings I believe that they lost
consciousness, a few phrases-eternal whistled into bottles or tapped
out on the bars without receiver, key, the code lost in the message.
What to do with the books? They wouldn't burn, not even doused
in gasoline, and so, ashamed, trying to save them from this last
humiliation, I threw them, smoldering, on a shroud, and dragged
them to the fields of wildflowers, waist-high by now, blown tidal
where I dug a hole and rolled them over and buried the books at sea.

TWO OF THE LOST FIVE
FOOLISH VIRGINS

I'd climb the ladder,
my eyes trained above
her head where the rope's
lashed to the harness
hook, and cut her down—
weep at the privilege.
My tears would not prevent
me from the task at hand.
I've lived, myself, this year
as long as she. The poetry's
no longer the vessel
it once was. Now it's
a wrist-thick mooring rope
fugitives grasp, hand over hand,
under cover of night
near launching, followed
by rats from dock to ship
who live on ballast grain,
grow strong through the long
crossing. But I'd rather
be the one to hold Tsvetaeva
as the rope is cut,
my strength tried awfully,
my arms around her
waist, my ear pressed against
her dead heart, breathing
her in. I'm old enough.
I have reason to imagine
we might recognize each other

and embrace, say in a flower
shop or walking by a river,
embrace as women do inside
the aftermath of youth,
its strange, enduring dust,
like two of the lost
five foolish virgins, once
so surprised at our delight
that we were turned away from
the bridegroom's door,
the oil in our lamps enough
to rub light into our faces,
gleeful in our sacrilege.
Delighted, oh yes—laughing
together at the memory,
pleased with ourselves—
that we were locked out,
turned back to the night
and its night people. I'd
rather be the one to hold
Marina as the rope's released,
as men suspend their women
in the dance and spin them
above the robbers' fires, the one
who holds her, heaves her
as the rope is cut, the one—
her age—who lays her down
and holds her head and rubs
the bloat out of her face

and smoothes her months-
worn smock over her knees.
Takes off her shoes. The one
who readies her and disappears,
leaving the burial to others.

How ever bad it was, she must have loved the dog, their walks by the
river. How the man who brought her here or what he thought no
longer mattered. Say she was spindrift. That's how it felt. Nothing
engaged her. Days went by before she'd bathe. She could smell the
animal like anguish in her hair and reveled in it. But for the dog she
might have hanged herself, or filled her pockets full of stones instead
of scraps for Cerberus. Two steps at a time she took the dark
staircases. Outside the gates, among the beggar dead, she'd find him,
kneel, unlock his chains. He leaned against her, as they walked,
his sphinx's shoulders. What he knew of her of course, no one can say.
Call it a nearness like a room you make inside yourself for sorrow.
Few are invited in. And she to him? Cerberus was welcome. In spring
among the trillium she longed for him. Who could believe it was a
pomegranate seed secured her soul? It was the dog that kept her
going back.

THE GARDENS OFFERED IN PLACE
OF MY MOTHER'S DYING

We emptied the books of songs
into rich soil, and all the prophets' names,
in honor of the gardener.

Evenings we studied catalogs and maps,
sketched out parterres, beds, lawns, savannahs,
chose as the guardian stone the flowering fire.

No garden need have walls, but we latticed the perimeters.
We planted broom, mock orange, yew, holly, boxwoods—
islands for the ancestors—
grouped them, let some stand alone.

We imported, improvised,
circled our feet with painted pebbles.

When the angle of the sun was right and moisture-laden,
the very air exaggerated aerial perspectives,
the light itself a pilgrimage

to all the years we'd been away that blew full and breathed
like wildflowers down the hillsides
brilliant with news, the throngs advancing.

O the whiter the light, the more we planted.
Everything grew then, everything flowered.
We nearly tired of singing inside such mortal clanging,
such festering, bell-ringing green

that we began to dream of miles of rock,
in our sleep scythed valleys or built a house on stilts
and sat above the tree line seeking out some distant plane—

what we saw against the screen of the horizon
likewise in the sky took dominion.

Yes, even sky became a garden.
The clouds banked west like Shiva's mountain.

We stood in the streets clapping our hands,
ran headlong down the sidewalks till such eternal,
insolent crows exploded from the park trees,

rode wing-wide the river thermals.

Then who could choose once and for all
between God's cities and the cities of Cain,
between Eden and the abundant weeds flowering among the ruins,
seeding themselves for miles

on the ledges of public buildings,
the hospital, effaced by windows,

ours lit all night, ten stories high,
framed and framing mere fragments of the natural.

Across the alley, above the fire escapes,
someone had painted roses.
Someone had dragged a mattress on a roof.

On a square of bright green carpet no bigger than a door
a table waited.

What did they see when they looked at us,
if they looked at all,
who were the chill inside a room in early spring,
or the dream so strange you might believe
that you inherit memory.

We were the boat in the distance
in the gardens on a plate, setting out beyond the blue bridge.

POMEGRANATE

O lovely matter, meager, half rotten,
I held a pomegranate once,
my hands cupped inside another's hands.

But I couldn't be loved like that,
locked song,
nor love,

who saved rooms in myself to dust for nothing,
nothing, that I might own
parts of myself

to squander or inherit,
as one inherits lemon groves,
fine feet,

a house of stone discovered in a wandering,
the table, the bed, pulled
also out of stone,

where I could live months away from my husbands!—
there sleep,
grow strange, of many minds inside a memory,

never to be relieved
of the burden of being,
nor changed,

nor taken up, not in this lifetime.
Glacial, the pomegranate,
my harbinger these brilliant, barren years—

scrotal you pomegranate,
given to long rot and yet too delicate,
recreant, a sack of stars.

DAMASCUS

Split by the light, wrought golden, one of a thousand cars stunned
    sun-blind,
crawling westward, I remembered a day I stopped for an old snapper,
as huge as, when embracing ghosts, you round your arms.
Who did I think I was to lift him like a pond,
or ballast from the slosh of hull swamp, tarred as he was, undaunted,
that thrashed and hissed at the worst place to try to cross,
where the road plunged east, the lumber trucks
swept daily down from the blue hills
past winter-ravaged toys blanching by makeshift crosses.
An old sea shimmered in the asphalt.
Spared over the mirage to ancient footpaths, he lunged again,
and spit, turning his oddly touching head toward the project
of the steep embankment. Such were the times.
Hardwired, the way. Cross here or die. Die crossing.

FENCE OF STICKS

As I was building a fence of sticks I heard the question,
Weren't there times worse than this for art?
Weren't there those who, rather, bristled were they *understood,*
who worked alone, the manuscripts thrown out or bled beyond the
    margins.
I was sewing the wire between the pine and sycamore,
tightening the warp with willow and forsythia, some just in bloom.
I thought of those who'd rather hang themselves than call truth
    heresy.
Upon whose deaths the citizens rejoiced.
They who burned everything.
Those who died longing to say more, whose heads rolled singing.
I was strict with myself, worked long past noon.
The gloves made the weaving hard so I wrought barehanded.
So many pages ending ＿＿＿, or neatly numbered, or written across
    the mind.
Those for whom art was not an occupation.
Indeed some never wrote again after what war or famine. Some wrote
    of nothing else.
I gathered the climbing roses' whips almost impossible to fit,
that made a lovely spiraling pulled taut, resisting,
each section a stay against the ocean of dead leaves.
A wind came up, the early heat unnerving. Those who refused to
    make it easy.
They who'd be damned to change a word. The way it came to them
so they would claim. The way was given. How heavy the lengths,
year after year, of pine boughs, Christmas wreaths brown to the bone,
red ribbons like a shout, like an embarrassment,
the holly sprigs still sharp as thorns. Those who died having said
    too much.

Or who must stop every few lines to dip the quill. They who ran out
    of time.
Those who ripped folios from the classics.
The boxwood leaves, like oaks', hold to the bough.
You must strip them by hand, yank the twigs backwards.
I took an ax to the twisted yew, blow after blow, and still it tore.
Its sap ruins this page. I had to pull myself away to write is this not
    happiness?

ACKNOWLEDGMENTS

Heartfelt thanks to my editor, Deborah Garrison; to my mother; my sisters Rena, Gena, Eve, Connie, and Beth; my brothers Everett, Paul, David, and Stephen; and to Jonathan Wilson for his enthusiasm and support of this work.

PERMISSIONS

Grateful acknowledgment is made to the following maga-
zines and anthologies in which many of these poems first
appeared: *Atlantic Monthly:* "Winter Barn," "Trapeze"; *Kenyon
Review:* "The Gardens Offered in Place of My Mother's Dying,"
"Lilacs," "Guillotine Windows," "Pomegranate," "Fence of
Sticks," "Telling the Bees," "Greeter of Souls"; *The New Yorker:*
"Boat," "Seersucker Suit"; *Salmagundi:* "Raising the Woolly
Mammoth," "Gown of Moleskins," "Solomon's Spoons,"
"Becoming a Poet."

"Winter Barn," "Lilacs," and "Guillotine Windows"
appeared in *The New Breadloaf Anthology of Contemporary
Poetry,* ed. by Michael Collier and Stanley Plumly (Middle-
bury College, 1999).

"The Rainbow Bridge in the Painting of the Sung
Dynasty," "Two of the Lost Five Foolish Virgins," and "Guil-
lotine Windows" appeared in *Poets of the New Century,* ed.
by Roger Weingarten (David R. Godine, 2001).

"Winter Barn," "Lilacs," "The Gardens Offered in Place of
My Mother's Dying," and "Guillotine Windows," appeared
in *Voices of Light, Spiritual and Visionary Poetry by Women
Around the World from Ancient Sumeria to Now,* ed. by Aliki
Barnstone (Shambhala, 1999).

Deborah Digges was born and raised in Missouri. She was the author of six collections of poetry and two memoirs. The recipient of grants from the John Simon Guggenheim Memorial Foundation, the National Endowment for the Arts, and the Ingram Merrill Foundation, Digges lived in Massachusetts, where she was a professor of English at Tufts University until her death in 2009.

A NOTE ABOUT THE TYPE

The text of this book was composed in Apollo, the first typeface
ever originated specifically for film composition. Designed by
Adrian Frutiger and issued by the Monotype Corporation of London
in 1964, Apollo is not only a versatile typeface suitable for
many uses but also pleasant to read in all of its sizes.

Composed by NK Graphics
Printed and bound by Offset Paperback Manufacturers,
Dallas, Pennsylvania
Designed by Virginia Tan